MONDAY MORNING INSPIRATION

CHRISTIAN INSPIRATION to OVERCOME
EVERYDAY MONDAY MORNING BLUES

DR. ANTIPAS L. HARRIS

HIGH BRIDGE BOOKS
HOUSTON

"In the morning, LORD, you hear my voice;
in the morning I lay my requests before you and wait expectantly."
—Psalms 5:3

DeShawna

Thank you!

This book is dedicated to my wife, Micah, a hard-worker who loves Monday mornings even when the "Monday morning blues" weighs heavy on her. I often see her reading Bible verses before she gets out of bed to start her day.

CONTENTS

ACKNOWLEDGEMENTS

TO GOD BE THE GLORY; great things He has done! I would like to thank all who subscribe to my Monday Morning Inspiration blogs and those who read the emails I send on Monday mornings. Your responses to the entries inspire me!

I would like to thank my wife, Micah, for your support and for your suggestions to make the blogs more reader-friendly. No one challenges me to think deeper than you!

I would like to thank my student, Brittney Lyons, for your help with proofreading and offering suggestions. God is using you to bring glory to His name!

I would like to thank Darren Shearer and the folks at High Bridge Books for believing with me that God will get the glory from another one of my publications.

May you, the reader, find inspiration in the words ahead. May your life become all that God intends. May you discover a daily dosage of encouragement that will help you deal with everyday life with a Christ-like attitude.

INTRODUCTION

HAVE YOU EVER HEARD the expression, "Monday morning blues?" The phrase speaks to a common reluctance to get up and go to work on Monday mornings. Already, I know that you can relate!

Oddly, however, Forbes contributor Stan Phelps cites research by Ipsos Public Affairs in which Phelps argues that Monday mornings may not be that "blue" for most people.[1] Ipsos Public Affairs surveyed 2,000 American employees, inquiring about their confidence in going to work on Mondays. Thirty percent of them reported that they are confident in going to work on Mondays. Twenty percent reported that they are stressed at the beginning of the week. Phelps surmises, moreover, that the notion of *Monday morning blues* might not be as normal as we think. The study shows that going to work on Mondays is a challenge that most people are eager to take on. They see Mondays as the first step to conquer their week.

So, what is that feeling that most of us can relate to when we think about "Monday morning blues?" The studies don't simply cause those Monday morning feelings to vanish away. Like you, when I first learned of the study, I was taken aback. I thought, *Something is wrong with that study! I know too many people who struggle with getting up in the mornings—every day for that matter.* Most people probably love their jobs and are grateful for life. But they struggle with some form of the "Monday morning blues."

Pondering the validity of the report in the face of lived experience, I investigated the meaning of the term, "Monday morning blues." What does it really mean? Perhaps, the studies that debunk the notion of the Monday morning blues are defining the experience differently than many people who claim to experience these feelings. What does "Monday morning blues" mean from a clinical perspective?

According to the *Encyclopedia of Sleep and Sleep Disorders*, scholars say that Monday morning blues is

> ...the feelings experienced at or soon after awakening on a Monday morning characterized by difficulty in awakening, tiredness, fatigue and grogginess... The sleep pattern shifts on the weekend causes difficulty in initiating sleep at an earlier time on Sunday night, resulting in a later-than-desired sleep-onset time. This is compounded by the fact that the time of arising on Monday is typically earlier than that which occurred on the prior weekend mornings. As a result, the total sleep duration prior to awakening on Monday morning is less than is required for full alertness.[2]

In other words, Monday mornings are indeed tough for many people due to shifts in normalcy and sleep patterns, not because people lack confidence in working, nor is it because people don't want to work. We live with a plate full of work but with less rest than we need and with an even greater deficit in personal devotion. As a result, we often are tired and drained when duty calls. All we have is desire; energy is often low. As a result, for some of us, even our confidence often is challenged.

Renowned cardiologist Chauncey Crandall reports on research at Tokyo Women's Medical University about the relationship between Monday morning blues and health. According to the study, 175 men and women were given a device to measure their blood pressure around the clock for a week. Astoundingly, the highest blood pressure readings registered among these working people occurred during the times that they were getting ready for work on Monday morning. Those who did not have to work and slept in longer didn't have the same upsurge in their blood-pressure readings.[3] Crandall adds, "Other studies have shown that there are 20 percent more heart attacks on Mondays than any other day."[4]

Early 20th-century African-American musician John Smith Hurt (1892–1966), also known as Mississippi John Hurt, recorded the blues song, "Monday Morning Blues." He defined the blues in a similar way as the *Encyclopedia of Sleep and Sleep Disorders* define it and consistent with Crandall's report on Monday morning stress research. On the recording before singing the blues song, Mississippi John Hurt gives this intro (with an African-American, Southern dialect):

Monday morning blues is something that all we working class people wake-up with some mornings. You know how it is; you stay up so late, and when you get that morning, when you get out the bed, first thing to go to work, you can't hardly find your Monday morning shoes.[5]

Then, Mississippi John Hurt proceeds to sing,

I woke up this morning, I woke up this morning,
Woke up this morning, with the Monday morning
    blues.

I couldn't hardly find, I couldn't hardly find,
I couldn't hardly find, my Monday morning shoes.

Monday morning blues, Monday morning blues,
Monday morning blues, searched all through my
    bones.

Monday morning blues, Monday morning blues,
Monday morning blues, made me leave my home.

Perhaps, the scholars could have just taken a lesson from the Mississippian, former-slave blues guitarist. Early Monday morning, challenges concerning our work are not always a dread. One may love one's job and still experience the toughness of getting up on Monday morning for various reasons. As the clinical definition says, it could be a result of changes in weekend sleep patterns. Also, for pastors and church volunteers, weekends may be busier than weekdays. Preaching and serving—for some of us, at multiple weekend services—can take a toll on the body. So, Monday mornings come with a physical demand for rest!

On another note, for those of us who wrestle with depression, anxiety, or insomnia, Monday morning blues is not restricted to Mondays. A Monday morning blues-type experience is an every-morning occurrence. More than ever, Americans try to cram too much in a day. We use up our resilience, piling more and more on our plates. We are fine until things go awry. A junk pile of stress weighs heavily on our shoulders. It will affect our bodies and minds. Life's stresses can take a toll on us and add to reasons for depression, anxiety, and insomnia.

Situations can throw some pretty hard blows. From personal hardships to systemic injustices; from personality conflicts at work to threats of national terrorism; many people lay down at night and wake-up each morning in fear, worrying about what's next. In this way, one may wake-up every day with what has been termed, "Monday morning blues." Where might one turn? Where might one draw strength to overcome the blues?

Prophetic literature teaches that the ultimate relief comes when one acknowledges the source of all comfort. Sometimes referred to as *prophetic liturgy*, Isaiah 33 paints a picture of God's people tyrannized by a "destroyer and traitor," probably Assyria. In their misfortune, the prophet leads Israel in an early-morning devotion. In part, he says, "O Lord, be gracious to us; we long for you. Be our strength every morning, our salvation in time of distress" (Isaiah 33:2). In Isaiah 35, the Lord responds with promises of renewal and peace.

The prophet joins a historical liturgical chorus of early morning devotions. Abraham had early morning time with the Lord. Genesis 19:27 states, "Now Abraham arose early in the morning and went to the place where he had stood before the LORD." In response to Abraham's prayers, God preserved his nephew, Lot, from the destruction of Sodom and Gomorrah.

Elkanah and Hannah worshiped early in the morning. 1 Samuel 1:19 states, "Early the next morning [Elkanah and Hannah] arose and worshiped before the LORD and then went back to their home at Ramah." God responded to their prayers and cured Hannah of infertility. Soon, she gave birth to Samuel.

David prayed a similar morning prayer when he faced the blues. Psalms 5:3 states, "In the morning, LORD, you hear my voice; in the morning I lay my requests before you and wait expectantly."

Our Lord Jesus Christ communed with the Father early in the morning. According to Mark 1:35, "In the early morning, while it was still dark, Jesus got up, left the house, and went away to a secluded place, and was praying there."

Early-morning sacrifice was part of the Hebrew worship ritual. Perhaps, God codified this ritual to help His people to get past the morning blues. But also, morning worship sets the tone for the day. It separates one from whatever worries or nightmares one endured during the night and initiates a fresh start. Morning devotions acknowledge that God is more powerful than whatever problems might arise during the rest of the day. They evoke God's justice in the face of insurmountable injustice and fear. Morning devotions are a statement to ourselves and to God that we cannot figure out our life's blueprint. We need the Master Architect to construct our lives to be all that God intends. Stated differently, morning prayer is our way of saying, "Lead me, Lord. I do not know the way to my destiny."

Growing up, our family had 5am prayer. It was the best thing that ever happened to me. Even today, I awake early and pray. At times, I tend to drift from this practice. But I continually must renew my commitment to early-morning prayer. Morning devotions are fundamental to coping with the pressures of life. They are foundational to maximizing life's potential. They are essential to dealing with the vicissitudes of life.

Devotions must include prayer. The pages ahead are complementary to prayer and must not replace it. I hope that you will hear God speak back to you through the pages ahead. Read one chapter a day after you pray. When you have read it, pray again.

May the words of my pen and the meditations of my heart be acceptable in your sight, Oh Lord!

Servant of the Lord Jesus Christ,
Antipas L. Harris

- Email: **info@antipasharris.com**
- Twitter & Instagram: **@drantipas**
- To learn more about Dr. Antipas L. Harris, go to our website, **www.antipasharris.com**.

1

IF GOD PUTS SOMETHING IN YOU...

What's in you is greater than where you are!

Did you hear about the rose that grew from a crack in the concrete?
Provin nature's laws wrong it learned how to walk without havin feet;
Funny it seems but, by keepin its dreams it, learned to breathe fresh air;
Long live the rose that grew from concrete when no one else even cared;
No one else even cared;
The rose that grew from concrete.

— from "The Rose that Grew from Concrete" by Tupac

HAVE YOU EVER THOUGHT, *I know that God put this gift, idea, vision, or desire in me, but I am struggling because the conditions I'm in right now are not favorable to bring it forth? I don't have adequate resources, support, or the right platform.*

If you ever have felt this way, Jesus' mother, Mary, can relate! This was her situation after carrying the baby Jesus for nine months. I recently re-read Luke's account of the birth of Christ. Luke 2:6-7 caught my attention:

> While [Joseph and Mary] were [in Bethlehem], the time came for the baby to be born, and [Mary] gave birth to her firstborn, a son. She wrapped him in cloths and placed him in a manger, because there was no guest room available for them.

Isn't it amazing that the Savior of the world was born in a small town and in a context of undesirable conditions?

Why would God choose a small town in the middle of nowhere for His only begotten Son's birth? After all, He is God! God created the whole earth. Why not a beautiful town with nature's beautiful gardens like Eden? One would think that God would choose a noble if not a notable location for this epic event. Yet, in God's divine irony, He chose an ignoble and insignificant small town for His Son's birth.

Adding to the narrative, there was no availability at the inn for Mary to deliver the baby in a decent room. The only option available to Mary was a nearby cave. And, the only bed in which she could lay the newborn was an animal feeding trough (manger).

Why would God allow His Son to be born in such humble conditions?

As I reflected on this story, the Spirit revealed to me that God does not need elaborate conditions to birth His glory!

To borrow Paul's words,

> But God chose the foolish things of the world to shame the wise; God chose the weak things of the world to shame the strong. (1 Corinthians 1:27)

What a lesson of encouragement to us! Many times, we may feel that our ideas are small or that our resources are limited. Even worse, we may feel that conditions are not favorable to birth the vision God has given to us.

Well, Jesus' birth narrative teaches us that significant limitations and unfavorable conditions create the right environment for revealing God's glory!

The people at the inn didn't know that Joseph didn't impregnate Mary; God did! Who would have thought that the baby born to the peasant girl actually belonged to God?

By comparison, who would think that God would birth something out of you that belongs to Him?

Don't let size and tough conditions dictate to you what God can bring out of you.

Don't allow closed doors to determine the value of what God places in you.

Let the naysayers talk. Let the lookers stare. Let the ones who could help but choose not to help go on their selfish way.

If God puts it in you, it does not matter where you birth it.

That baby lying in the animal-feeding trough on that solemn night in Bethlehem would one day fulfill God's promise of salvation to the world!

God is able to use you to make a global impact, regardless of where you start.

Will you allow him?

We join with the entire world that, for centuries, has marveled at Jesus' birth. In David's words, "The LORD has done this, and it is marvelous in our eyes" (Psalms 118:23). So, if God puts something in you, it does not matter where you birth it. Just bring it forth in due season wherever you are. God gets glory through unprecedented challenges. What is in you is greater than where you are!

TAKE A MOMENT TO REFLECT

Where are the places in your life where you are struggling with the call of God?

_____

_____

_____

_____

_____

Regardless of your limited resources, what are some steps you can take to seize this moment in your life?

_____

_____

_____

_____

_____

2

CHOOSE PEACE...

O a little talk with Jesus make it right, all right
Little talk with Jesus make it right, all right
Troubles of ev'ry kind
Hank God I'll always find
That little talk with Jesus make it right.

My brother, I remember when I was a sinner lost
I cried, "Have mercy, Jesus"
But still my soul was tossed
Till I heard King Jesus say,
"Come here, I'm on the way"
And little talk with Jesus make it right.

Sometimes the fork lightning and muttering thunder, too
Of trials and temptations
Make it hard for me and you
But Jesus was a friend,
He'll keep us to the end
And little talk with Jesus make it right.

My brother and my sister, you have trials like me,
When we are trying to serve the Lord
And win the victory
Old Satan fight us hard

Our journey to retard
But little talk with Jesus make it right.
— *"A Little Talk with Jesus"*, *Negro spiritual*

I WAS ON A ROUTINE, five-mile, Saturday-morning walk when I heard the Holy Spirit say, "Peace is a choice." In other words, God's peace is not contingent upon life's circumstances. It is the situation of a mind that focuses on the things of God and a soul that rests in Him. The prophet Isaiah said,

> You (God) will keep in perfect peace those whose minds are steadfast, because they trust in you. (Isaiah 26:3)

Where is your mind? And, who do you trust?

In the New Testament, the Apostle Paul was thrown into prison for preaching. From his cell, Paul wrote a letter to his Philippian congregation, teaching them about the power of divine peace in troubled times. Paul asserted,

> And the peace of God, which surpasses all understanding, will guard your hearts and your minds in Christ Jesus. (Philippians 4:7)

What overwhelming promise! God does not promise us that troubles will not come. But, He offers peace to guard our hearts and minds from the unending clutches of sorrow and the hopeless, ravishing anguish of devastation.

A practical example would be the 19th-century, young lawyer, Horatio G. Spafford, and his wife. They had five children.

Their youngest child and their only son got sick and died at four years old.

On November 21, 1873, Mrs. Spafford and their four daughters went from Chicago to Europe on a family trip. Horatio was to join them a few days later after settling a business matter.

Mrs. Spafford and the four girls were among approximately 313 people onboard a ship that wrecked in the Atlantic Ocean. Of the five Spaffords aboard the ship, only Mrs. Spafford survived.

When Horatio heard the news, he rushed to his grieving wife's side in Europe. According to Mr. and Mrs. Spafford's daughter (Bertha Spafford Vester), who was born after the tragedy, the ship's captain (who was carrying Horatio to Europe) pointed out to him the place in the ocean where his four daughters drowned.

As Spafford leaned over the side of the ship with grief pouring from his heart, his mind was filled with the words of this song:

> When peace like a river attendeth my way,
> When sorrows like sea billows roll,
> Whatever my lot, Thou hast taught me to say,
> It is well, it is well with my soul.

The Spafford story is deeply moving in so many ways. A series of catastrophes descended upon this family and disrupted what was once a thriving, highly-respected Christian life. Similar to the biblical story about Job, all that the Spaffords had was gone! Yet, they discovered a deep peace in their souls, this Christ-centered peace that surpasses understanding.

What a peace!

Spafford's hymn continues to bless millions of people today. More importantly, may we choose the peace of Christ that Spafford chose.

TAKE A MOMENT TO REFLECT

In what areas of your life do you find yourself wrestling in the absence of peace?

_____

_____

_____

_____

_____

_____

_____

What needs to be removed or reconstructed in your life in order for you to experience the fullness of God's peace?

_____

_____

_____

_____

_____

_____

_____

3

JUST DO GOD...

I'm gonna sing when the Spirit says sing,
I'm gonna sing when the Spirit says sing,
I'm gonna sing when the Spirit says sing,
and obey the Spirit of the Lord.

I'm gonna pray when the Spirit says pray,
I'm gonna pray when the Spirit says pray,
I'm gonna pray when the Spirit says pray,
and obey the Spirit of the Lord.

I'm gonna moan when the Spirit says moan,
I'm gonna moan when the Spirit says moan,
I'm gonna moan when the Spirit says moan,
and obey the Spirit of the Lord.

I'm gonna shout when the Spirit says shout,
I'm gonna shout when the Spirit says shout,
I'm gonna shout when the Spirit says shout,
and obey the Spirit of the Lord.

—"I'm Gonna Sing," Negro spiritual

MY COUSIN, PAT DIXON, ONCE CALLED and encouraged me with these words during the course of our conversation: "Antipas, just do God."

I hadn't heard such a phrase before. It sounded good, but I was not sure of what "just do God" meant.

However, lately, I have been thinking about how important it is to do what God says to do.

That's it! To obey God is what it means to "just do God!"

Have we forgotten the Christian virtue of *obedience?* In a world wherein "doing what we want and how we want" has become the order of the day, Christians find it challenging to submit to God's way when what He says is contrary to what we want to do.

Early-Church father, Bishop Ignatius, once said,

> It is a great delusion in those whose understanding has been darkened by self-love, to think that there is any obedience in the subject who tries to draw the superior to what he wishes.

In other words, obedience means we must sacrifice our own lusts or desires and submit to God's will.

Even Jesus prayed,

> Father, if you are willing, take this cup from me; yet not my will, but yours be done. (Luke 22:42)

Our Lord demonstrated the virtue of obedience in the recognition that God's will is likely to be inconsistent with our own.

We must not become so consumed by the fight for our rights that we fail to remember that there is such a thing as submitting to God's way with self-abandonment.

I have a long way to go on this, indeed.

In fact, we can't arrive at obedience on our own. We need the power of the Holy Spirit.

The Spirit empowers us to obey God. The prophet Isaiah said,

> If you consent and obey, You will eat the best of the land; "But if you refuse and rebel, You will be devoured by the sword." Truly, the mouth of the LORD has spoken. (Isaiah 1:19-20)

From experience, obeying God flies in the face of fleshly desires. That's how we know it's God! When God speaks, we never want to do it. We toss and turn, wrestling with ways to justify doing something differently. But that voice sticks with us even when we choose to disobey. In the long-run, however, we wish we had listened to God. God speaks to us in alignment with our best interest even when we don't think He is.

Oh, how we need the power of the Holy Spirit to live in a way that not only pleases God but also brings long-term joy in our lives!

I invite you to pray the words penned by the notable 19th-century preacher, Charles H. Spurgeon:

> Lord sanctify us. Oh! That Thy spirit might come and saturate every faculty, subdue every passion, and use every power of our nature for obedience to God.

Let's remember how important it is to walk in obedience. But, we need God to empower us to "do God."

Come, Holy Spirit. Help us to "just do God!"

Take a Moment to Reflect

What are your personal desires or wants that are contradictory to what God has predestined for you?

In what ways have you expressed obedience to God? In what ways have you expressed disobedience to God?

4

SEEK TO PLEASE GOD...

Don't work so hard.

Hold to His hand,
God's unchanging hand;
Hold to His hand,
God's unchanging hand;
Build your hope on things eternal;
Hold to God's unchanging hand.

   —*"Hold to His Hand," traditional African-American*
    song

"Jesus said to him, 'Receive your sight; your faith has
healed you.'"

   —*Luke 18:42*

"And without faith it is impossible to please him [God],
for whoever would draw near to God must believe that he
exists and that he rewards those who seek him."

   —*Hebrews 11:6*

HAVE YOU EVER tried so hard to please God through acts of righteousness, but all of your efforts sent you into one tiresome tailspin after another?

I know that feeling!

The more we work to fulfill righteousness, either the more unrighteous we discover that we are, or we resort to self-righteousness to make ourselves feel better.

Neither situation is God's best for us.

The author of *Hebrews* relieves us with this good news: we do not have to work so hard to please God.

Pleasing God is a matter of faith. Seeking God is a matter of faithfulness.

When we faithfully seek God, we live by faith and not works. Our own acts of righteousness are but as filthy rags, anyhow (see Isaiah 64:6).

Faith teaches us that the power of God's righteousness is fulfilled in us through Christ's finished work on the cross (see Romans 8:3-4).

Madame Jeanne Guyon was a 17th-century laywoman whose spiritual experiences and writings speak to our need to let go and let God work in us. Guyon wrote,

> When the torrent begins to lose itself in the sea, it can easily be distinguished... So the soul, leaving this degree, and beginning to lose itself, yet retains something of its own; but in a short time it loses all that it had peculiar to itself...
>
> The soul sees now that whatever it owned formerly had been in its own possession; now it no longer possesses, but is possessed: it only takes a new life in order to lose it in God; or rather it only lives with the life of God; and as He is the principle of life, the soul can want nothing. What a gain it has made by all its losses! It has lost the created for the Creator, the nothing for the All in all. All things are given to

it, not in itself but in God; not to be possessed by itself, but to be possessed by God. Its riches are immense, for they are God Himself. It feels its capacity increasing day by day to immensity; every virtue is restored to it, but in God.[6]

In other words, without Christ, we can do nothing (see John 15:5)!

However, as the old saying goes, "We have skin in the game." Our role is to trust that Jesus did it for us and to remain committed to the cause of Christ in faith, hope, and love.

Let's stop trying so hard, slow down, and keep it simple. Let's rest in God's power to empower us to walk by faith in Christ rather than in our own works.

Take a Moment to Reflect

In this social media age, do you spend a lot of time trying to win likes?

Are there places in your life where you are trying to make God love you more? It is not necessary! God loves you unconditionally. Believe and receive God's acceptance.

5

EVERYTHING ELSE WILL FAIL...

Hold on to Jesus.

You better get a home in that rock,
Don't you see;

You better get a home in that rock,
Don't you see;

Between the earth and sky,
I can hear my Savior cry;

You better get a home in that rock,
Oh, don't you see;

Rich man died he lived so well,
When he died he got a home in hell;

Poor man Lazarus poor as I,
When he died he got a home on high;
You better get a home in that rock.

    —"You Better Get a Home in that Rock",
      Negro spiritual

LIVING IN A HOME AWAY FROM HOME, African-American slaves had to adjust to the harsh realities associated with the force of displacement and brutal treatment.

Where do you find a sense of belonging when you do not belong? How do you adapt to neighborhoods that reject your humanity?

All the slaves really had was their newfound faith in Jesus Christ. It was the religion that their slave owners purported. They really did not have much of a choice. But, as it turned out, finding Jesus was the best thing that could have happened to the slaves.

Ironically, the slaves transferred their deep sense of African spirituality into their newly-discovered faith in Jesus Christ. They worshipped God from the depths of their souls. They built a relationship with the Lord in their everyday, life experience through singing and dancing. Their expressed spirituality through song and dance left behind theological nuggets on which we can build our faith.

The spiritual, "I've Got a Home in that Rock", reveals that—in the homeless-type reality of slavery—the slaves learned that the only true refuge is in Jesus Christ. It is hard to grasp this important lesson when we are not in a distressed situation.

Contemporary Christians often measure God's favor based on attaining material things. A message that associates "getting money and stuff" with the favor of God has entangled much of popular Evangelical Christian theology. Indeed, God does bless people with things. However, if we are not prayerful, nice-paying jobs, comfortable homes, and nice cars will spoil us into thinking that material possessions are the epitome of God's blessings.

The slaves offer to us sound doctrine:

> You better get a home in that rock,
> don't you see;

You better get a home in that rock,
don't you see;
Between the earth and sky,
I can hear my Savior cry;
You better get a home in that rock,
Oh, don't you see.

Undoubtedly, the slaves observed that some of their wealthy masters seemingly had everything to make a comfortable life, but they were often unhappier than many of the slaves. They resolved that true refuge and divine favor have more to do with a conscious choice to live a life in Christ than with the temporal happiness that wealth brings. As stated in the subtitle of a report by the American Psychological Association, "Religion may fill the human need for finding meaning, sparing us from existential angst" (Beth Azar, December 2010).

The slave message is consistent with Azar's findings. The slaves' Christian doctrine teaches that, when we encounter life's inevitable vicissitudes, the comfort of nice homes will give way to the discomfort that stress brings. Nice cars will breakdown. Money cannot buy joy. Riches cannot buy eternal needs. The slaves' sapient theology goes like this:

Rich man died he lived so well,
When he died he got a home in hell;
Poor man Lazarus poor as I,
When he died he got a home on high;
You better get a home in that rock.

Take a Moment to Reflect

Is there anything in your life that you have prioritized more than God?

_____

_____

_____

_____

_____

_____

_____

What have you found yourself seeking security in?

_____

_____

_____

_____

_____

_____

_____

6

LORD HELP ME TO STAND

So many falling by the wayside,
Lord help me to stand;

So many falling by the wayside,
Lord help me to stand;

So many falling by the wayside,
Lord help me to stand;

Take me by my hand,
And lead me on.

—Dorothy Love Coates

ISN'T IT INTERESTING that, when we first came to the Lord, we felt like we could change the world? I have talked to so many people who started the journey full of excitement and fervor to share the good news. I call this the "mountain-top experience". It's when you are so on-fire for God that even Monday mornings start off great.

Inevitably, somewhere along the way, the excitement for Jesus gives in to what seems like the Passion of Christ. That is when the "rubber hits the road." The life of Christ is not meant to be utopia. It is meant to be a sort of fuel to keep going amidst the vicissitudes of life. Paul affirms the reality of Christian struggles when he says to Timothy, "Indeed, all who desire to live a godly life in Christ Jesus will be persecuted" (2 Timothy 3:12).

The joy of going through life as a Christian is that we are not alone! Jesus said, "In this world you will have trouble. But take heart! I have overcome the world" (John 16:33b).

What a blessing!

The enemy will intensify attacks through temptations, adversity, and struggles. Some of them will be an onslaught of external forces. Others will be battles in our minds. Yet, we can find comfort in knowing that Jesus is with us. He will help us to stand firm in faith as well as to keep our sanity regardless of the challenges.

Our responsibility is to remain faithful to Christ through our struggles. Jesus keeps His promise to remain with us. Will we remain with Him?

Take a moment to reflect on these words from 20th-century German theologian Dietrich Bonhoeffer, who aptly explained,

> The messengers of Jesus will be hated to the end of time. They will be blamed for all the division which rend cities and homes. Jesus and his disciples will be condemned on all sides for undermining family life, and for leading the nation astray; they will be called crazy fanatics and disturbers of the peace. The disciples will be sorely tempted to desert their Lord. But the end is also near, and they must hold on and persevere until it comes. Only he will be blessed who remains loyal to Jesus and his word until the end. (from *The Cost of Discipleship*)

TAKE A MOMENT TO REFLECT

Have you lost your joy in the journey of faith?

_____

_____

_____

_____

_____

_____

_____

Are you faithful to all that God has called you to be and do?

_____

_____

_____

_____

_____

_____

_____

7

ARE YOU STUCK, LOOKING BACK AND TALKING ABOUT THE PAST?

Ain't gonna let nobody turn me 'round,
Turn me round, turn me 'round.
Ain't gonna let nobody, turn me 'round.
I'm gonna keep on a-walkin', keep on a-talkin',
Walkin' into freedom land.

—*"Ain't Gonna Let Nobody", Civil Rights song*

INDEED, GOD HAS DONE great things. We must never forget to Praise the Lord for what He's done.

Can I share some good news? The Lord has even more in store for you!

Look back, and appreciate God for what He has done. But, don't just keep looking at what used to be. God wants you to look forward to what He is doing and to what He will do in your life.

This week, live with greater expectation!

Indeed, God's Word never changes. God's truth is enduring. His mercy is everlasting. Yet, God is bigger than what we've seen Him do in our lives. Truth is so much bigger than what we've known. God is greater than what we've experienced. There's so much more!

Isaiah 43:18–19a states, "Forget the former things; do not dwell on the past. See, I am doing a new thing! Now it springs up; do you not perceive it?"

You may think that the deck seems to be stacked against you right now. Perhaps, you spend too much time reflecting on the past glory days and wishing those "good-ole-days" would come back.

God is able to take every obstacle and make them stepping stones for the springing up of even more glorious days. He'll help you to beat the odds through Jesus Christ and rejoice in something new.

Do *you* perceive it?

Get ready for what you haven't experienced in God. Get ready to learn what you don't already know about God's power.

Don't linger in the past. Open up, and receive God's new thing. God will do greater acts in your life and through you for others.

Do *you* perceive it?

Let's live with great expectation!

Let the words of this contemporary song take rest in your heart today:

Expecting great things
I'm expecting great things
I'm using my faith, and I'm expecting great things

Know that God has much in store
Exceedingly, abundantly more and more and more

Expecting great things
I'm expecting great things
I'm using my faith, and I'm expecting great things

(from "Expecting Great Things," Veronica Petrucci)

TAKE A MOMENT TO REFLECT

Is there anything negative in your past that you find yourself dwelling on?

_____
_____
_____
_____
_____
_____
_____

What has God promised you that has not come to pass, yet? Be encouraged, and continue to believe God for what He promised He will do.

_____
_____
_____
_____
_____
_____
_____

8

GOD CHOSE ME FOR NOW...

What's the plan?

I've been kissed by God, I've been hurt,
I've been marked for death, almost ripped apart...
But the sirens had never woke me,
Only reason I'm here now is cause God chose me.

—*"God Love Us" by Nas*

SO MANY THINGS RUN in and out of our minds each day. It's easy to get lost in our thoughts. If we are not careful, we will forget to recognize that the very breath we breathe is a blessing. While we might not have all that we wish we had, stuff is not the most important. What's important is that God has given to us life, health (even if we are sick), and strength (even when we are weak). And, that's a blessing!

Our prayers must be of praise and worship to God more than we make requests of God. As the old adage goes, "If it had not been for the Lord on our side, where would we be?" The saying is lifted from Psalm 124:

> If it had not been the LORD who was on our side—let Israel now say—if it had not been the LORD who was on our side when people rose up against us, then they would have swallowed us up alive, when their anger

was kindled against us; then the flood would have swept us away, the torrent would have gone over us; then over us would have gone the raging waters. Blessed be the LORD, who has not given us as prey to their teeth! We have escaped like a bird from the snare of the fowlers; the snare is broken, and we have escaped! Our help is in the name of the LORD, who made heaven and earth.

God has chosen you and me to be alive at this time in history. It's important that we cooperate with God's choosing. We must be attuned to the Holy Spirit to know our purpose. More importantly, we must walk in it. It is easy to complain about our felt needs. But, the more important question should be, "What does God want me to do?"

There is an old song that my great aunt used to sing at church growing up:

> So glad I'm here, (hallelujah) I'm so glad I'm here;
> So glad I'm here in my Jesus name;
> So glad I'm here, (hallelujah) I'm so glad I'm here;
> So glad I'm here in my Jesus name;
>
> Gonna serve while I'm here, gonna serve while I'm here;
> Gonna serve while I'm here in my Jesus name;
> Gonna serve while I'm here, gonna serve while I'm here;
> Gonna serve while I'm here in my Jesus name;

Just as God told Jeremiah that He knew him before forming him in his mother's womb (Jeremiah 1:5), God also knew us before forming us. Before we stepped into this world, God placed purpose in us. When we recognize the blessing of God's purpose for us being here, it is so much easier to be thankful. The question becomes, *What is God's plan for our purpose?* Let's seek God for the plan, and walk in it!

TAKE A MOMENT TO REFLECT

Have you ever questioned whether you have a purpose? If so, what led to this doubt?

_____

_____

_____

_____

_____

How can you begin to implement God's purpose in your life on a daily basis?

_____

_____

_____

_____

_____

9

LOVE IS THE ANSWER...

Share love in action!

So close your eyes and you can feel it
Comin' straight from above, it's the power of love
You can't deny it, so don't even try it
Let the feelin' sweep you off your feet

You've got to believe in love
It's a feeling that's next to none
Can't stop until we are one
With the power of love

Tell everyone you see
How much better the world could be
For them and for you, for me
With the power of love

> *—from "The Power of Love" by Marcus Miller and*
> *Luther Vandross*

THE WORLD IS FULL of possibilities. Yet, hate competes with the chances to build the global family that God intends. Lately, I have been questioning what single virtue might change the world.

Paul says, "And now these three remain: faith, hope and love. But the greatest of these is love" (1 Corinthians 13:13).

Twentieth-century African-American mystic and theologian Howard Thurman explained that "love of the enemy means that a fundamental attack must first be made on the enemy status." In other words, love defies the concept of "enemy." Martin Luther King, Jr. aptly noted that "love is the only force capable of transforming an enemy into a friend."

Have you ever felt that more people are against you than for you? It seems so much easier to fight back, matching wrong with wrong. But, love is a way of being as well as a way of acting in the world. Love's actions match wrong with righteousness, converting the resistant activity of the would-be enemy into the silent acceptance of friendship.

God wants us to live out the power of love. As Martin Luther King, Jr. put it, "Love transforms." In *Romans*, Paul echoes his sentiments on love's transformative nature: "If your enemy is hungry, feed him; if he is thirsty, give him something to drink. In doing this, you will heap burning coals on his head" (Romans 12:20; also, Proverbs 25:21–22).

In his book, *Jesus and the Disinherited*, Howard Thurman explained,

> The religion of Jesus says to the disinherited: "love your enemy." Take the initiative in seeking ways by which you can have the experience of a common sharing of mutual worth and value. It may be hazardous, but you must do it.[7]

It is possible to share mutual worth and value without accepting improper or unrighteous behavior. Often, we reject others because we reject their ways. There is a difference!

We cannot change people's behavior, but love can. We must only focus on loving. Love affirms people. When our love is pure, it increases our quality of life. In other words, we are happier when we love. We see life in a positive light when we love. We make the world a better place by expressing love despite the hate, bigotry, animosity, and vindictiveness that tempt us to do otherwise.

How can you show love today? Love has a way of changing people's attitudes and their way of dealing with us!

The challenge for us this week is to think of genuine ways to shock someone with love. Repeat the effort over and over. Let's see what irresistible, transformative love can do!

TAKE A MOMENT TO REFLECT

In what ways has God shown undeserving love to you?

_____

_____

_____

_____

_____

_____

_____

Do you have people in your life who you consider enemies? If so, how can you express love to them in a way that would convert their negative attitude toward you and win them to friendship? Be creative!

_____

_____

_____

_____

_____

_____

10

THE POWER OF THE WAIT...

Hold on to God.

Hold on just a little while longer
Hold on just a little while longer
Hold on just a little while longer
Everything will be alright
Everything will be alright

— *"Hold on", Negro spiritual*

ONCE, PASTOR JIM WOOD of First Presbyterian Church of Norfolk and I co-taught a Wednesday-night Bible study. Our topic was "Power of the Wait." We explored scriptural teachings about waiting on God. We learned that waiting on God has to do with the human soul being grounded in Christ.

It is one thing to expect God simply to answer our prayers the way we want Him to. It is another matter to wait on God, believing that, even if God does not come through when we want or in the way we want, God remains the only source for which all humanity yearns.

It is a wonderful thing to find God. Hallelujah!

Yet, faithfulness to God means we must abide in Him. Keep waiting on God even when life gets frustrating—it will!

Waiting on God is part of what it means to depend on Him despite the odds. Pentecost happened in Acts 2 while the people of God were waiting on Him. If the Church was born out of faithfully waiting for the coming of the Holy Spirit, Christians must continue to wait in faith, believing that God will come through for us in God's way and in God's timing.

The 19th-century Underground Railroad Conductor, Harriet Tubman, often prayed this prayer: "Lord, I'm going to hold steady onto You, and You've got to see me through." In other words, waiting on God is not a passive way of living. It means to depend on God actively whether in needing something from God, in decision making, or in acting in accordance with God's will for our lives.

Yet, waiting on God means we must act in sync with God's timing. Bishop T. D. Jakes rightly explained,

> Timing is so important! If you are going to be successful in dance, you must be able to respond to rhythm and timing. It's the same in the Spirit. People who don't understand God's timing can become spiritually spastic, trying to make the right things happen at the wrong time. They don't get His rhythm—and everyone can tell they are out of step. They birth things prematurely, threatening the very lives of their God-given dreams.

At the Bible study, Jim and I discussed Simone Weil, a faithful, early-20th-century believer. Weil was a young, French woman who struggled with physical illness most of her life. She died at the young age of 34, but Weil left behind some keen wisdom for Christian thought and practice. Let's ponder and live out these words from Weil: "To be rooted [in Christ] is perhaps the most important and least recognized need of the human soul."

With our feet planted in faith in Christ, let us wait on God with an "anyhow" kind of faith.

TAKE A MOMENT TO REFLECT

Are there broken areas in your life that you are depending on God to fix? Have you been trying to manipulate the outcome of those areas?

Waiting on God requires patience. In what ways can you exercise patience during the wait?

11

I'VE GOT A FEELING EVERYTHING'S GONNA BE ALRIGHT...

Just gotta let God do it!

I've got a feeling everything's gonna be alright,
I've got a feeling everything's gonna be alright,
I've got a feeling everything's gonna be alright,
Be alright, be alright, be alright.

—*"Everything's Gonna Be Alright"*, *Negro spiritual*

IF YOU ARE LIKE ME, when things go wrong, your mind goes into "fix-it" mode more often than "prayer mode." Even when we go through "prayer motions," our minds often are hard at work, trying to figure things out.

I am learning, however, that while human ingenuity is capable of many things, there are some things that are beyond human ability to figure out and fix. In fact, our limited abilities are not our own anyway. It is God who works in us to do what we are able to do. Yet, the grace of God sets limits on our abilities, or else we never would have a reason to turn to God.

You probably have heard it said, "Our extremity is God's opportunity." I have quoted this many times. But, when the rubber hits the road, it is challenging to simply "let go and let God handle it."

Hymnist Joseph Medicott Scriven was spot-on when he wrote,

> O what peace we often forfeit,
> O what needless pain we bear,
> All because we do not carry
> Everything to God in prayer!
> (from "What a Friend We Have in Jesus")

Too often, we substitute joy with sorrow, peace with worry, and faith with doubt. Ralph Waldo Emerson wisely noted, "Sorrow looks back. Worry looks around. Faith looks up."

We must pull ourselves together and believe that God has our best interests at heart. He "is able to do immeasurably more than all we ask or imagine, according to his power that is at work within us" (Ephesians 3:20).

In other words, "Let go, and let God work it out!"

TAKE A MOMENT TO REFLECT

Are you worrying about things you can't control?

How can you trust God more?

12
WHAT DOES IT REALLY MEAN TO WIN?

My true believers, fare ye well,
Fare ye well, fare ye well,
Fare ye well, by de grace of God,
For I'm going home.

Massa Jesus give me a little broom
For to sweep my heart clean,
And I will try, by de grace of God,
To win my way home.

—"Fare Ye Well", Negro spiritual

LIFE SEEMS FILLED with competitions. The question lingers, Who will win? For me, this question has morphed into another, broader theological question: What does it mean to win? Or better, What does it mean to win as a child of God?

Comparing athletics with winning as children of God, Paul explained,

> Everyone who competes in the games goes into strict training. They do it to get a crown that will not last, but we do it to get a crown that will last forever.
> (1 Corinthians 9:25)

The promised, enduring crown symbolizes the ultimate meaning of life in Christ. In Christ, we are winners!

Elaborating on winning Christ's way, Slave Christians explained their view of Christ-related victory in the song, "Fare Ye Well."

> Massa Jesus give me a little broom
> For to sweep my heart clean,
> And I will try, by de grace of God,
> To win my way home.

This stanza suggests two important insights. The first is that winning is birthed out of relationship with Jesus Christ. Jesus has what it takes to win, and our participatory relationship with Him is crucial to what it means to win.

King David asked a rhetorical question of related concern and followed-up with a response of similar resolution:

> How can a young person stay on the path of purity?
> By living according to your word. (Psalms 119:9)

Reading the lyrics in the spiritual through the lens of the *Psalms*, we learn that the Word of God is the "little broom" (in the spiritual) we need for heart cleansing. So, it is prudent that we meditate on the Word daily.

Secondly, Christian slaves associated heart-cleansing with the highest form of winning. For them, to win a place of belonging with Jesus is what it means to win.

It is of utmost importance to learn that the Christian's life journey is a faith journey. We need Jesus to help us to make it to the finish line.

Amidst life's competitiveness, be encouraged that the faith journey is a race all of us can win; it is a non-competitive race. It is not about who gets there first. The winners are anyone who perseveres through the vicissitudes of life just to get there. We are in different places in our journeys. Let's keep moving.

The writer of *Hebrews* put it this way:

> ...let us throw off everything that hinders and the sin that so easily entangles. And let us run with perseverance the race marked out for us, fixing our eyes on Jesus, the pioneer and perfecter of faith. For the joy set before him he endured the cross, scorning its shame, and sat down at the right hand of the throne of God. (Hebrews 12:1-2)

Get up, and get dressed. Get ready to win with Jesus!

TAKE A MOMENT TO REFLECT

Do you allow yourself time each day to meditate on God's Word?

How can you strengthen your personal relationship with Jesus?

13

LET JESUS BLESS YOU...

One day, one day, while walkin' along,
Jesus don bless my soul;

I heard a voice an' saw no one,
Jesus done bless my soul.
O go an' tell it on de mountain,
Jesus done bless my soul;

O go an' tell it in de valley,
Jesus done bless my soul.

He done bless my soul an' gone to glory, Good Lord,
Jesus done bless my soul;

Done bin here an' bless my soul an' gone on to glory,
Jesus done bless my soul.

—"Jesus Don Bless My Soul", Negro spiritual

OFTEN, WE ASK GOD to bless our pockets with money, our homes
with material things, our careers with promotions, and our name
with favor. Although these things are of earthly benefit, they are
fleeting. Money comes and goes, material things will fade away,

and favor is temporal. The most important blessing that we can have is a "soul blessing."

The soul is eternal. When all else fades, the soul is that inner person that will remain. The soul will stand before God and give an account of all we have done, valued, not done, and not valued. God has a vested interest in the state of the soul and extends Himself to comfort, sustain, and redeem our souls.

Late 15th century devout Christian Catherine of Genoa's *Spiritual Dialogue*, she shares her spiritual experience wherein the body and soul had a conversation:

> I saw the Body and Soul conversing and arguing with one another. And the Soul said: God made me to love and to be happy. I should like, then, to start out on a voyage to discover what I am drawn to. Come willingly with me, for you too will share my joy.[8]

Indeed, when our flesh submits to the soul's search for God, we find the fullness of peace. Elaborating on the journey of the soul, the Psalmist said,

> Truly my soul finds rest in God; my salvation comes from him. (Psalms 62:1)

The Savior offers to us an important reasoning concerning the value of our souls:

> What good will it be for someone to gain the whole world, yet forfeit their soul? Or what can anyone give in exchange for their soul? (Matthew 16:26)

Moreover, while we work hard, build careers, grow bank accounts, and enjoy the goodness that life has to offer, let us remember to spend time with Jesus. Let us talk to Him throughout the day as we go about our daily duties. He will listen to us and will speak to us. He will guide us in decision-making and strategies for our lives. He will correct us where we are wrong. Most importantly, as we walk and talk with Jesus, He will bless our souls!

TAKE A MOMENT TO REFLECT

How can you invest more time with Jesus every day?

Do you find yourself seeking most of your pleasure in material things?

14

EVERY DAY IS A DAY TO GIVE THANKS!

Lord I just want to thank you.
Lord I just want to thank you.
Lord I just want to thank you.
Lord I just want to thank you.
I want to thank you
for being so good to me, so good to me.

You were my bread when I was hungry.
You were my bread when I was hungry.
You were my bread when I was hungry.
You were my bread when I was hungry.
I want to thank you
for being so good to me, so good to me.

—"Lord, I Just Want to Thank You!", traditional
African-American church song

HAVE YOU EVER BEEN waiting for the phone to ring or for an email to come? The good news that we desperately want to hear often just does not come fast enough. But, we worry that maybe the news might not be so good when we get the call or when the email finally comes through.

What a stressful feeling!

I have been there so many times. If we are not careful, we will look back and discover that we spent far too much time worrying about what we wanted and far too little time offering thanks. Second-century Greco-Roman philosopher Epictetus once said, "[S]he is a wise [wo]man who does not grieve for the things which [s]he has not, but rejoices for those which [s]he has."

When we focus on what we want, it is easy to lose sight of the joy of the moment. It is also easy to take our eyes off the current assignment. We become vulnerable to missing out on the quality relationship with the Lord we could have now.

Helen Keller was blind and deaf. Her work inspires me when I am feeling angst about life. Helen wrote,

> I thank God for my handicaps. For through them, I have found myself, my work and my God.

Wow!

How can someone whose life activity seems so limited give thanks to God in the middle of such challenges?

Let Helen Keller's words convict our hearts to spend more time thanking God rather than complaining. While we await the next news, let's spend time giving thanks that things are as well as they are.

In the 1600s, a Christian Frenchwoman named Jane de Chantal devoted her life to encouraging the sick and poor. She built eighty-six homes for them. De Chantal left letters, some of which explained the power of giving thanks amidst very difficult times. In one of her letters de Chantal said,

> As for the will of God's good pleasure, which we know only through events as they occur, if these events benefit us, we must bless God and unite ourselves to

this divine will which sends them. If something occurs which is disagreeable, physically or mentally, let us lovingly unite our will in obedience to the divine good pleasure, despite our natural aversion.... Whatever good or evil befalls you, be confident that God will convert it all to your good. (Annecy, 8 May 1625)[9]

De Chantal's words echo Paul's teaching that we should,

Give thanks in all circumstances; for this is God's will for you in Christ Jesus. (1 Thessalonians 5:18)

Admittedly, it is hard to express thanksgiving when life serves a blow at our hearts. May the Lord Jesus help us to find the strength to offer thanksgiving in the good times and the bad times. We can only do this by God's grace.

TAKE A MOMENT TO REFLECT

What are situations that you worry about more than give thanks?

How can you incorporate a thankful attitude in your relationship with God?

15

HEALING BELONGS TO GOD...

Sometimes I feel discouraged and think my work's in
    vain,
But then the Holy Spirit revives my soul again.
There is a balm in Gilead to make the wounded whole;
There is a balm in Gilead to heal the sin sick soul.
If you cannot preach like Peter, if you cannot pray like
    Paul,
You can tell the love of Jesus and say, "He died for all."
There is a balm in Gilead to make the wounded whole;
There is a balm in Gilead to heal the sin sick soul.
Don't ever feel discouraged, for Jesus is your friend;
And if you lack for knowledge, He'll never refuse to lend.
There is a balm in Gilead to make the wounded whole;
There is a balm in Gilead to heal the sin sick soul.

    —"There is a Balm in Gilead", Negro spiritual

WE EXPERIENCE MANY physical, emotional, and psychological hurts in life. Sometimes, we live with the pain such that we give up on hope for healing.

No one has known pain like the African-American slaves. I do not think that the books and movies really can capture the level of hurt many of them experienced. Yet, Slave Christians found hope in the Scripture and sang their conviction:

There is a balm in Gilead to make the wounded
   whole;
There is a balm in Gilead to heal the sin sick soul.

When I consider the throbbing realities of social ills, the aching hearts that don't seem to heal, and the vicious diseases that seem incurable, my mind is clouded with despair. But, when I think about who Christ is, my heart leaps with the hope of His healing power.

Christian slave theology affirms that Jesus is our friend and source of healing. His healing is full and complete. Jesus is the only balm of healing. No need to search for another. We must pour out our hearts to God in Jesus' name and let the healing begin.

In *Matthew*, we read of the healing power of Jesus Christ:

Great crowds came to him, bringing the lame, the blind, the crippled, the mute and many others, and laid them at his feet; and he healed them. The people were amazed when they saw the mute speaking, the crippled made well, the lame walking and the blind seeing. And they praised the God of Israel. (15:30-31)

Jesus is still healing in the world today—no matter the sickness. Jesus has the power to heal all manner of sickness and disease.

Take a Moment to Reflect

Is/are there any area(s) in your life where you need the healing touch of Jesus? The areas could include physical, emotional, psychological or otherwise.

_____

_____

_____

_____

_____

_____

_____

_____

In what ways will you be a walking testimony of God's healing power?

_____

_____

_____

_____

_____

_____

_____

_____

16

GOD'S STILL CHANGING LIVES...

I know I've been changed;
I know I've been changed;
I know I've been changed;
angels in Heaven done signed my name.
Well if you don't believe that I've been redeemed,
you know the (angels in Heaven done signed my name);
oh follow me down to that old Jordan stream,
angels in Heaven done signed my name.

I stepped in the water and the water was cold,
you know the angels in Heaven done signed my name;
oh it chilled my body but not my soul,
angels in Heaven done signed my name.

—"I Know I Been Changed" by LaShun Pace

I WAS AT THE BARBER SHOP. A man (I will call him *Bob*) was there playing chess with my barber when I walked in. When my barber came to cut my hair, the other man, whose back was turned to me, turned around. I recognized him from a local church. He was a minister!

Soon, the minister shared his testimony with the men in the shop. I was moved deeply as he took us through his life's journey.

Bob said that, several years ago, he was a habitual robber, cocaine addict, drug pusher, and a womanizer. He went into details explaining how, in the early 1990s, he robbed houses of VCR players and sold them to support his habits. He told of how close he came to death.

Bob found himself in jail, trying to figure life out. Most importantly, he wanted to just do his time and get out to hit the streets again. Bob was not concerned about doing the right thing. He was concerned about getting caught and how he could do "better" at getting by.

Bob said that, one day, another inmate came by his block and asked if he wanted to go down to the church service that was getting started soon.

Bob shrugged his shoulders and told the fellow inmate, "Leave me alone." The guy left him alone.

The next week, the fellow inmate dropped a Bible off at his cell block. Bob saw the Bible and, being nice to him, said, "Thanks, Man."

A few days later, Bob decided to open the Bible to read it for the first time in his life. He had gone to church as a young boy but never read the Bible. This experience was life-changing!

Soon, Bob gave his life to Jesus. He testified that his life had not been the same since. Today, Bob is a minister of the gospel!

My heart leaped!

It is great to hear that a life has been changed in jail. But more importantly, Bob's change was not merely "jailhouse religion." It was the real thing!

Be encouraged that God is still changing lives!

Let this testimony be an inspiration to you. Perhaps, you are struggling with an addiction. Or perhaps, you are struggling with the misperception that your life must remain in a setback. Or, maybe it's not you, but it's a loved one or a friend.

Setbacks are a reality. Thank God for being a God of change.
Get ready for the comeback.
God still changes lives!

TAKE A MOMENT TO REFLECT

Is there an area in your life that you need God to change?

_____

_____

_____

_____

_____

_____

Pray for the areas in your life where you need change. Also, write down some names of people you know to be in need of the changing power of Jesus Christ.

_____

_____

_____

_____

_____

_____

17

CHASING AFTER GOD...

Running, running, running,
I can't tarry;
Running, running, running,
I can't tarry;
Running, running, running,
I can't tarry;
Running up the King's highway.

> —*"Running, Running, Running", traditional*
> *African-American congregational song*

"I seek you with all my heart; do not let me stray from your
commands."

> —*Psalms 119:10*

HAVE YOU EVER BEEN in a place wherein you felt desperate for God? It was not that you believed God was far away. But, life's situations had piled so high that there seemed to be nowhere to turn for solutions or resolutions.

Material gains are not sufficient, and you are tired of talking about the challenges you face. You feel that you need God desperately.

As recorded in the *Psalms*, the sons of Korah felt this way, too. They wrote,

As the deer pants for streams of water,
so my soul pants for you, my God.
My soul thirsts for God, for the living God.
(Psalms 42:1–2a)

To chase after God speaks of a deep desire for God in desperate times.

Growing up, we used to sing a gospel song that depicts the soul's yearning for Him.

Running, running, running,
I can't tarry;
Running, running, running,
I can't tarry;
Running, running, running,
I can't tarry;
Running up the King's highway.

Jesus is the King, who cares for each of us and responds to our hearts' earnest cries. Chasing after God does not assume God is not present. It means that our hearts—or, as the Psalmists put it, our *souls*—are in earnest pursuit of God. Chasing after God is a posture that admits,

We need Thee; Oh, how we need thee;
Every hour we need Thee.

David said,

From the ends of the earth I call to you, I call as my heart grows faint; lead me to the rock that is higher than I. (Psalms 61:2)

Let's chase after God with all of our hearts. Jesus said and says to us now,

Come to me, all you who are weary and burdened, and I will give you rest. (Matthew 11:28)

The Lord takes joy when we pursue Him. If we seek Him with all of our hearts and souls, we will discover hope to endure through the challenges we face.

TAKE A MOMENT TO REFLECT

What can you do specifically to pursue God every day?

_____

_____

_____

_____

_____

_____

_____

Is there anything hindering you from pursuing God with your whole heart?

_____

_____

_____

_____

_____

_____

_____

18

JESUS IS REAL...

Real, real; Jesus is real to me,
Oh, yes, He gives me the victory;
So many people doubt Him,
But I can't live without Him;
That is why I love Him so,
He's so real to me.

   —"Real to Me", author unknown

I HAVE FOND MEMORIES of growing up in Manchester, Georgia. We went to church four or five times a week. For the first hour or so of service, we had what we called "Devotional Service." The first hour or more was filled with spontaneous singing and prayer. Sometimes, we had what we called "Testimony Service" during the Devotional Service. Other times, Testimony Service was separated from the Devotional Service and placed after the preaching.

The late Mother Laurel Hartnett was a mother at the church who frequently sang during the Devotional Service. One of her favorite songs was "Real, Real; Jesus is Real to Me." If Mother Hartnett didn't sing this song enough, my mom would lead the same song. It was always a powerful worship experience. As they led the song, others would join in singing "Real to Me."

The lyrics were simple. In the African spiritual tradition, the chorus repeats over and over for about five minutes or more. We sang the words with intense conviction. In the African tradition, repetition causes the stirring of the Spirit. The more we repeated "Real, Real; Jesus is real to me…" the more convicted we became that what we were singing was indeed true: Jesus is real!

For us, the issue was not whether or not Jesus was a historical figure. That was a foregone conclusion. Our confession was a theological one: Jesus is indeed God!

We couldn't argue scientific rationales for the existence of God, but our souls witnessed to an experience with One who is greater than us. When we called on Jesus, He responded to us. The simple things in life verified for us the realness of our Savior.

We didn't have a lot of material possessions. But, when we called to Jesus, He answered with food to satisfy our hunger. We didn't have a lot of money. But, when we needed provision, we prayed in Jesus' name. He responded with necessary provision.

Our experiences with the living Lord taught us that what the Bible says about Jesus is true. We added another chorus of conviction: "You can't make me doubt Him. I know too much about Him."

We often testified that Jesus is greater than doubt, fear, and agony. Whatever we were going through at the time disappeared in the simple but profound testimony that Jesus is real.

You may not know biochemistry and trigonometry. You may not read Greek and Hebrew. But, let's consider our simple experiences that bear witness to what the Bible says. Let's get to know Jesus and share the testimony: "Real, real. Jesus is real to me!"

As you start your day, repeat these words over your day,

Regardless of the doubts I face today, one thing I will hold on to; that is Jesus is real.

Indeed, we serve a living Savior who is in the world today. He is alive and willing to help us through life's ups and downs. Jesus is real; God really loves us.

TAKE A MOMENT TO REFLECT

What is your first memory of learning who Jesus is?

How will you help others see that Jesus is real?

19
GOD OF THE *IN BETWEEN*....

Oh, Mary, don't you weep, don't you mourn;
Oh, Mary, don't you weep, don't you mourn;
Pharaoh's army got drown-ded;
Oh, Mary, don't you weep;
Moses stood on the Red Sea shore;
Smotin' the water with a two by four;
Pharaoh's army got drown-ded.
The Lord told Moses what to do
To lead those Hebrew children through.

—"Oh, Mary, Don't You Weep", Negro spiritual

ALL OF MY LIFE, I have heard that God is Alpha and Omega, the Beginning and the End. So, it was clear in my mind that God is the Maker of the universe, and wherever the end of it may be, God has that under control as well. I have heard that Jesus is the Author and the Finisher of the Faith. For me, this means that Jesus is the founder of Christianity, and He will complete any need for Christian maturity in the Christian's life.

Beyond these broad theological concepts, life is full of beginnings and endings, starts and finishes. The Christian believes that God is there in the beginning and will be there in the end. While this is common Christian belief, the question resides in *the in between*. That is where most of the fear happens.

There are many *in betweens* in life. Whether it's *in between* graduation and the next phase of life, *in between* jobs, *in between* promise and fulfilment of promise, *in between* a prophecy and its coming to reality, or *in between* relationships, the *in between* is a tough place. It's where you hate that you ever left where you were.

In my journey, however, I have learned that *in between* the beginning and the ending is where I need most of my help, encouragement, and support. It occurred to me that many people don't even start journeys of desired destinies because they become comfortable with the familiar, even if it's chaotic.

When many of us start the journey, leaving the past puts us in a vulnerable place. While the past was undesirable, at least, we knew what to expect and learned to deal with the expected. But, being between the past and the future puts us in a vulnerable place. Stress, lots of pain, the unexpected, and fear of the unknown happen in this vulnerable place, the *in between* place.

The *in between* place was the wilderness experience for Israel. They did not like Egypt. But, it was familiar. It was very hard for them to live in Egypt but even harder to leave. They wanted the promise of a Land that flowed with milk and honey, but they did not want to deal with the process to get to that promise. The process is the *in between* place.

Moses struggled to convince the people of God to leave slavery. When he did, they ended up in the wilderness for much longer than they should have been there because they could not seem to let go of the attitudes and lifestyles they had adapted to in Egypt. They could not take their past into the future. But, it was hard for them to embrace a new reality for fear that it might not work for them. Their vision was blurred in the *in between* place, so much so that they concluded that Moses had brought them into the desert to die.

Sometimes in our lives, our vision for the future is blinded by our fear of letting go of the past in the face of current challenges. In many cases, we rather would hold on to slavery than to let go for fear that the future will let us down. We must remember that our mechanisms of safety in the past really did not keep us safe. It was the Alpha, the Author of our Faith who kept us then. And, that same God is also the Omega, the Finisher of our Faith.

Even more importantly, I have learned along with Israel that God is also the God of the *in between*. This means that God cares about where we are right now: the wilderness experience. He will not fail us. He will not forsake us. We safely can let go of the past and depend on the God who is *in between* the past and the future.

Like the Slave Christians, we can look back to what God did in the past to build our faith for what God is able to do now and later. They sang,

Oh, Mary, don't you weep, don't you mourn;
Oh, Mary, don't you weep, don't you mourn;
Pharaoh's army got drown-ded;
Oh, Mary, don't you weep;
Moses stood on the Red Sea shore;
Smotin' the water with a two by four;
Pharaoh's army got drown-ded.
The Lord told Moses what to do
To lead those Hebrew children through.

The Slave Christians took counsel from how God supported and sustained Israel in the wilderness. It stirred up their spirit of faith to believe that God would take care of them as well.

Remember today that our God is Alpha and Omega, the Beginning and the Ending; Jesus is the Author and the Finisher of our Faith. But also, Jesus is Lord of the *in between*. That's where we are not where we used to be but also not where we need to be. It can be stressful *in between*. We need grace because we will misstep at times. We need faith because this is a place of water-walking. Let's invite God's presence to be with us *in between*.

TAKE A MOMENT TO REFLECT

Where are the in between places in your life right now?

_____

_____

_____

_____

_____

In what ways will you be persistent in engaging God while in your in between place?

_____

_____

_____

_____

_____

20

DON'T LET THE DEVIL STEAL YOUR WITNESS

My soul is a witness for my Lord;
My soul is a witness for my Lord;
My soul is a witness for my Lord;
My soul is a witness for my Lord.

—"Witness for My Lord", Negro spiritual

THERE IS A FASCINATING passage in Revelation 12:11:

They triumphed over him by the blood of the Lamb and by the word of their testimony.

This passage follows the Apostle John's dramatic vision of Satan's assault against humankind. The Apostle explains that Satan wants to lead the whole world astray. Yet, God gives the solution that cripples the devil's agenda: the blood of Christ and telling our testimonies.

Wow!

Christ's death on the cross purged our sins away. When we receive what God did for us in Christ, we can live without guilt.

John (the Baptist) saw Jesus coming toward him and said, "Look, the Lamb of God, who takes away the sin of the world!" (John 1:29)

We are washed in the blood of Jesus. What a testimony! Hallelujah!

Also, the Cross of Christ expresses God's vicarious sacrifice for us. This means that we do not have to die in sin. Jesus already died for us. His death makes it possible for us to live.

Paul wrote,

And he died for all, that those who live should no longer live for themselves but for him who died for them and was raised again. (2 Corinthians 5:15)

When we come to know what Jesus did for us, we must live it and tell it.

Although slaves in American history, the Slave Christians tapped into a freedom that could not be constrained. That was the inner freedom that comes with knowing Jesus.

The Slave Christians boldly declared, "I am a witness for my Lord." They understood that bearing witness to Christ was a lifestyle as well as proclamation of the Faith. Such bold confession was deeply connected to their victory over the vicious life associated with American slavery. Their victory was rooted in their witness for Jesus.

When we live and tell our witness for the Lord, indeed, it communicates who we are. But more importantly, our testimony is part of what it means for us to gain the victory that comes with the Christian life.

The more we bear witness for Christ, the greater victory we experience. The Christian life was never meant to be a closet religion.

Could it be that, too often, we keep our Faith to ourselves?

Keeping it to ourselves defeats the purpose as well as stifles our ability to experience the fullness of the Christian life. The purpose of the blood of Christ is to bring salvation to the whole world. As Paul said, "Those who live [as witnesses to Christ] should no longer live for themselves but for him who died for them…" This means that Christ requires us to live in a way that bears witness to the fullness of what it means to have the risen Christ living in us.

When we live out our witness for Christ, we not only communicate Christ's best for the world, but we also expand our involvement in victorious living.

Revelation 12:11 promises triumph over Satan's agenda in our lives by the blood of Christ and through our witness.

Let's own our lives in Christ through the way we live and the conversations we have with others.

Take a Moment to Reflect

Is there anything in your life—presently or from the past—that you have been reluctant to use as a testimony to God's glory?

_____

_____

_____

_____

_____

_____

_____

What is your testimony? What has God done for you that others need to witness? Remember this: your testimony may help other people discover victory in Jesus.

_____

_____

_____

_____

_____

_____

_____

21

THE LORD'S SIDE... THE WINNING SIDE

Over'; on the Lord's side;
Over'; on the Lord's side;
Over'; on the Lord's side;
I'm glad I'm over; on the Lord's side.

—*"Over' on the Lord's Side", African-American*
congregational song

THERE IS NO DENYING THAT evil exists alongside God's work in the world. While the Devil is messing, God is blessing. And God's blessings are more powerful than whatever the Devil is trying to do!

The Devil speaks enticing words and drags us low as a means of manipulating our minds. Satan's agenda is to impede upon God's relationship with humankind. This was true in the Garden of Eden, and it is true today.

The Devil is jealous of God. But Satan cannot compete with God because he cannot create like God. So, the Devil seeks to demoralize that which God has created.

In other words, we are Satan's key targets because we were created in God's image. This is why God invites us into a deeply-rooted relationship through Jesus Christ. Jesus says, "Come to me, all you who are weary and burdened, and I will give you rest" (Matthew 11:28).

Have you ever paused to think about how amazing it is that, of all that God created, He offers to humanity the privilege of resting in Him.

Take a moment, and experience the awe of God's invitation.

When we think about it, we'll realize we do not have to worry so much. We were created in God's image. Though we are victims of Satan's deception of Adam in the Garden of Eden, Jesus has defeated Satan's scheme. Jesus offers to us the opportunity to live in total rest.

Humanity's greatest weariness is a result of separation from God. But our loving God invites us to re-enter His likeness through Jesus.

What a wonderful experience to accept Christ's gift!

Growing up, my dad (a pastor) often led our congregation in singing,

> Over'; on the Lord's side;
> Over'; on the Lord's side;
> Over'; on the Lord's side;
> I'm glad I'm over; on the Lord's side.

Dad was glad to be on the Lord's side because being with Jesus brings fulfilment. After all, this is where we were created to be: on the Lord's side! On the Lord's side, we can live out our purpose as God's image-bearers. Also, you and I can walk with a sense of belonging, a sense of destiny.

We also can employ our gifts and talents in a way that pleases God!

Have you ever felt that, because of poor choices you've made in the past as well as your ongoing challenges, you are a loser?

Many of us attune to that inner voice that speaks negatively of our future based on what happened in the past. If we are not careful, merely listening to that repeating voice of negativity can create a world of failure.

Every day is a fight.

But the question becomes, *Whose side are you on?* The only side of the fight of life that will win is the Lord's side.

I once met a 103-year-old man, an evangelist whose name was Bishop (Dad) Otis Clarke. What a wonderful man! He was active and on fire for the Lord. I had the opportunity to travel and minister with Dad Clarke in the Bahamas, Connecticut, Georgia, Texas, and in his home state of Oklahoma. Dad Clarke was well known for his wise words that bear repeating daily:

> It don't matter what the Devil say. He's a liar! When you get on the Lord's side, you are on the winning side! Get on the Lord's side, and you are a winner! [sic]

Are you on the Lord's side?

If your answer is *yes*, then you are a winner! Don't let those voices in your head convince you otherwise!

Listen to the words of the Lord, and rejoice that you are on the Lord's side!

> You are the salt of the earth. But if the salt loses its saltiness, how can it be made salty again? It is no longer good for anything, except to be thrown out and trampled underfoot. (Matthew 5:13)

When you are on the Lord's side, your house, your neighborhood, your community, your town, your city, your region, your nation, and the entire world are blessed because you are part of the Lord's army!

Hold your head up, and stay on the Lord's side.

In due time, everyone will see that this is the winning side!

TAKE A MOMENT TO REFLECT

Write out every negative thought that tries to keep you from moving into your future. Renounce them, and choose each day to think positively on purpose.

_____

_____

_____

_____

Make positive confessions that remind you each day that you are on the Lord's side. (Example: I am a child of God!)

_____

_____

_____

_____

22

SET THE ATMOSPHERE...

Excitement is contagious.

I get joy when I think about,
What He's done for me;
I get joy when I think about,
What He's done for me;
You can't tell it, let me tell it,
What He's done for me
You can't tell it, let me tell it,
What He's done for me.

> **—"I Get Joy", traditional African-American call-and-response song**

"Enthusiasm is one of the most powerful engines of success. When you do a thing, do it with all your might. Put your whole soul into it. Stamp it with your own personality. Be active, be energetic, be enthusiastic and faithful, and you will accomplish your object. Nothing great was ever achieved without enthusiasm."

> **—Ralph Waldo Emerson**

I USED TO BE A CHOIR DIRECTOR. Once the choir got their vocal parts right, we were ready to make music. Getting the parts right and making music are not the same.

What do I mean by "make music," you may ask?

Making music has to do with creating an atmosphere with the art of sound. Music really only happens where there is enthusiasm!

It's what Emerson meant when he described enthusiasm as "putting your soul into it!" It is the difference between existing and living. People who are not enthusiastic about life are not really living up to their maximum potential. Enthusiasm creates the atmosphere not only in making music but also in making a life out of existing.

Living with enthusiasm enlivens our surroundings. It is influential! One's enthusiasm initiates a sort of dance with others much like African indigenous "call-and-response" singing.

Call-and-response singing ignited communal hope that sustained African slaves as well as African Americans during the Jim Crow era. Call and response is when a leader sings one verse and the chorus answers with another verse.

The dancing-together approach to singing in call and response stirs-up the Spirit. If there was sadness before, it has been replaced with joy! Before you know it, there is an atmosphere of communal joy filled with dancing and praise.

By God's grace, we have the fortitude to create the atmosphere that brings life to others. You can set the atmosphere in your home, school, job, and community! It's probably easier than you think.

The way that we think will develop within us what we need to exude excellence, not only in our lives but in our surroundings.

Paul was incarcerated in Rome for preaching the gospel. Yet, from his prison cell, Paul penned one of the most inspirational letters of the New Testament to the Church in Philippi. Philippians 4:8 gets at the heart of the message here:

Finally, brothers and sisters, whatever is true, whatever is noble, whatever is right, whatever is pure, whatever is lovely, whatever is admirable—if anything is excellent or praiseworthy—think about such things.

What have you been thinking about? Our days are as good as our thoughts. Growing up, we used to sing the call-and-response song,

I get joy when I think about,
What He's done for me;

We cannot enjoy God's goodness without thinking about them. We cannot set the atmosphere around us with soul-stirring inspiration if we don't take initiative to think about positive things.

Think about the good things the Lord has done. Think about how fearfully and wonderfully God has equipped you with talents and gifts, talents and gifts you still are discovering and sharpening daily.

Remember, the way you think will determine what mood you exude. Even the worst ones of us resent negativity. We lead, and we create positive outcomes—first, through the way we think. Think truth, nobility, righteousness, purity, loveliness, and admirable things. Then, you will create awesome possibilities.

Even more, your enthusiasm about awesomeness will cause others to dance with you!

Take a Moment to Reflect

What do you spend your time thinking about?

_____

_____

_____

_____

_____

_____

_____

On a normal day, what kind of mood do you set when you walk into a place?

_____

_____

_____

_____

_____

_____

_____

23

BE AN OUTLIER...

Don't worry about trying to be somebody else.

He made me, What I am;
He made me, What I am;
He made me, What I am;
Jesus made me, What I am.

> —*"He Made Me What I am", African-American*
> *traditional congregational song*

OFTEN, CHRISTIANS FALL into jealousy because we either want what someone else has or want to be another person. It is so easy to covet what someone else has or try to imitate someone we admire.

Growing up, we used to sing the call-and-response chorus, "He Made Me, What I Am", as a celebration of our newfound appreciation for life in Christ. Too often, we sing the song but forget who we are in Christ. Jesus said,

> You are the salt of the earth. But if the salt loses its saltiness, how can it be made salty again? It is no longer good for anything, except to be thrown out and trampled underfoot. You are the light of the world. A town built on a hill cannot be hidden.
> (Matthew 5:13-14)

Because of Jesus Christ—regardless of our ethnic origin, social status, age, or gender—we are valuable. Our identity is in Christ. This means we are royal. Peter said,

> You are a chosen people, a royal priesthood, a holy nation, God's special possession, that you may declare the praises of him who called you out of darkness into his wonderful light. (1 Peter 2:9)

It is one thing for someone else to note our royalty. It is another to own it ourselves and walk in it.

Malcolm Gladwell explained that success is a gift. He said,

> Outliers are those who have been given opportunities—and who have had the strength and presence of mind to seize them.[10]

Our greatest opportunity is to live into the royalty that we have in Christ.

Could it be that you are too busy looking at someone else's value that you do not see your own?

Could it be that your baggage from the past has weighted you down so much that you cannot see how special you are?

Could it be that the confines of your current situation have limited your perception of how great God is?

God is King of the universe. Psalms 24:1 states,

> The earth is the LORD's, and everything in it, the world, and all who live in it.

As children of God, we are joint-heirs with Christ. This means that we are royal! To borrow words from Gladwell,

Now multiply that sudden flowering of talent by every field and profession. The world could be so much richer than the world we have settled for.[11]

Let's look to God who made us the unique gifts we are to the world. Celebrating his own uniqueness, the Psalmist wrote,

I praise you because I am fearfully and wonderfully made; your works are wonderful; I know that full well. (Psalms 139:14)

With the Palmist, may we celebrate our uniqueness and get going in fulfilling all that God has for us, not being envious of others.

Take a Moment to Reflect

What unique gift or talent has God given you?

How are you living out your God-given uniqueness?

24

TURN IT OVER TO JESUS…

Stop worrying about it.

---

*Like a ship that's tossed and driven, battered by an angry
    sea;*
*When the storms of life are raging, and their fury falls on
    me,*
*I wonder what I have done, that makes this race so hard
    to run;*
*Then I say to my soul, take courage (don't worry), the
    Lord will make a way somehow.*

*The Lord will make a way somehow, when beneath the
    cross I bow,*
*He will take away each sorrow, let Him have your
    burdens now;*
*When the load bears down so heavy the weight is shown
    upon my brow,*
*There's a sweet relief in knowing the Lord will make a
    way somehow.*

Try to do the best in service, try to do the best I can;
*When I choose to do the right thing evil's present on every
    hand;*
*I look up and wonder why that good fortune passed me
    by;*
*Then I say to my soul, be patient, the Lord will make a
    way somehow.*

Often there's misunderstanding, out of all the good I do;
Go to friends for consolation, and I find them
complaining, too;
So many nights I toss in pain, wondering what the day
will bring;
Then I say to my soul, take courage (don't worry), the
Lord will make a way somehow.

—"The Lord Will Make a Way Somehow" by Thomas
A. Dorsey

ARE YOU A WORRY WART? Do you know anyone who is?

At times, worry becomes a poor claim on prayer. Sometimes, we substitute praying with worry.

I'm learning that worry is a form of fear and doubtful impatience. Problems are less stressful than worry makes them out to be. People who do not worry so much tend to live with a better quality of life.

Living worry-free does not mean the same as living carelessly. Worry has to do with trying to fix things by our own strength. Carelessness means that we refuse to take responsibility for life's challenges.

Both worry and carelessness work against Christian progress!

We can overcome worry. The key is learning to turn our problems and concerns over to Jesus through constant prayer. When we take our burdens to the Lord, we must train ourselves to leave them in His hands. His hands are bigger and stronger than ours. The Lord is able to solve our problems and to address our concerns.

David said of the Lord,

> Because you are my help, I sing in the shadow of your wings. I cling to you; your right hand upholds me. (Psalms 68:7-8)

David, not only a man of God but also a warrior and king, understood that his success was neither in worrying nor carelessness. David maintained his sanity and was able to overcome the many troubles he faced through total dependence on the Lord.

As problems come, if we do not turn them over to the Lord for His wisdom and guidance, we will end up worrying about something that we cannot handle on our own. With patience and prayer, we can overcome much of the stress that we endure.

Julian of Norwich, a 15th-century Christian teacher, sums up worry as two sin sicknesses: impatience and fear. She said,

> God showed me two kinds of sickness that we have, of which he wants us to be cured. One is impatience, because we bear our labor and our pain heavily. The other is despair, coming from doubtful fear... these are two secret sins, extremely busy in tempting us. Therefore, it is God's will that they should be known, and then we shall reject them as we do other sins.[12]

Stress is a silent killer. It contributes to depression and fatal, health-related problems. In an article, "Stress: The Killer Disease" in *Psychology Today*, physician and psychiatrist Emily Deans explained,

Stress Kills. We've heard it before. It's common sense. But how does stress kill? As a physician, I tend to imagine stress leading to high blood pressure and heart attacks and anxiety or depression... Through a healthy lifestyle, good wholesome nutrition, and stress reduction, you can sometimes ameliorate the long term damage.[13]

We cannot control the problems that come our way. If we could pick and choose them, I am sure we would choose the ones with the least impact. But that is just not the way life goes.

While we cannot choose our problems, with the Lord's help, we can choose whether to worry or not.

Today, let's make up our minds not to worry. In the words from Thomas A. Dorsey's song,

> Say to [our] soul[s], take courage (don't worry), the Lord will make a way somehow.

TAKE A MOMENT TO REFLECT

Do you consider yourself to be one who worries often?

Has stress impeded upon your physical health? If so, in what ways? Pray and release the burdens to the Lord. Leave them with Him!

25

IT'S NOT ABOUT US…

To God be the glory!

To God be the glory;
To God be the glory;
To God be the glory,
For the things He has done;
With His blood, He has saved me;
By His power, He has raised me;
To God be the glory,
For the things he has done.

   —from "My Tribute" by Andrae Crouch

WHAT ARE YOU LIVING FOR? Why does it all matter? These are important questions that have rung throughout the corridors of human history. The 17th-century Westminster Catechism provides a sound response:

> Man's chief end is to glorify God, and to enjoy him forever.

Our most complete joy is found in glorifying God. When we live to glorify God, we discover purpose and fulfillment. There's no greater joy than the joy of being in communion with Jesus

Christ. My cousin, Michael E. Mathis, celebrates the life of Christ in his song, "The Best Life":

> This is the best life, living for Jesus;
> Soon, one day we'll be with Him eternally.
> This is the best life, living for Jesus;
> I'm glad to be a part of the family of God.

When we discover the richness that the Christian experience brings, we're able to live out the fullness of God's best. But it doesn't start with us. The life of Christ begins and ends with God. David said,

> Know that the LORD is God. It is he who made us, and we are his; we are his people, the sheep of his pasture. (Psalms 100:3)

What a blessing to be part of God's family!

God cares for you and me. He is with us even when others walk away.

Because of Jesus, we don't have to walk alone. He is with us through the tough times as well as the easier times. In fact, we wouldn't be who we are without the Lord. Let's not forget that!

The Lord has brought us safely this far and will carry us on. He is an excellent, heavenly Father who loves us.

Great is His faithfulness!

God's love brings us through the wilderness seasons of life. The Lord opens doors that otherwise would not have been opened to us.

Bless His name!

It's important to note that life with Jesus does not evade reality. It helps us to weather the storms. Considering David's own adversity and Israel's collective history, David expressed glory to God in this way:

> If the Lord had not been on our side—
>   let Israel say—
> if the Lord had not been on our side
>   when people attacked us,
> they would have swallowed us alive
>   when their anger flared against us;
> the flood would have engulfed us,
>   the torrent would have swept over us,
> the raging waters
>   would have swept us away.
> Praise be to the Lord,
>   who has not let us be torn by their teeth.
> We have escaped like a bird
>   from the fowler's snare;
> the snare has been broken,
>   and we have escaped.
> Our help is in the name of the Lord,
>   the Maker of heaven and earth. (Psalms 124)

Can you think of times when you almost gave up, but God stepped in?

If it had not been for the Lord on our side, where would you and I be?

To God be the glory!

In Andrea Crouch's song, "My Tribute," he adds, "And if I gain any praise, let it go to Calvary."

Praise the Lord!

TAKE A MOMENT TO REFLECT

In what ways has God shown faithfulness to you?

_____

_____

_____

_____

_____

_____

_____

How are you giving God glory for the things He has done for you?

_____

_____

_____

_____

_____

_____

_____

26

I Shall Not Be Moved…

I shall not, I shall not be moved;
I shall not, I shall not be moved;
Like a tree planted by the water;
I shall not be moved.

When my cross is heavy, I shall not be moved;
When my cross is heavy, I shall not be moved;
Like a tree planted by the water;
I shall not be moved.

If my friends forsake me, I shall not be moved;
If my friends forsake me, I shall not be moved;
Like a tree planted by the water;
I shall not be moved.

—"I Shall Not Be Moved", Negro spiritual

TENACITY IS AN IMPORTANT Christian value. Often, it seems much easier to give up than to keep going. Have you ever sanctified the temptation to give up by saying, "I don't think God wants me to do this?" Of course, there are many things that God does not want us to do. But God speaks clearly. No need to use challenge as a litmus test to determine God's will.

My greatest challenges often come in the direction in which God is leading. But I have learned that, if something is God's will and I stick with God, neither the Devil nor Hell itself can stop, block, or destroy what God is doing. Isaiah 14:27 declares,

> For the LORD Almighty has purposed, and who can thwart him? His hand is stretched out, and who can turn it back?

Could it be that there are times when we are our own greatest hindrances? Jesus had a conversation with a group of people who held up a boatload of excuses for why they couldn't follow Him. All of their excuses seemed to make sense. For example, Jesus had nowhere for them to lay their heads. One of them had death in the family. Another one wanted to follow Jesus but was concerned about kinfolk. Luke 6:57-62 recounts Jesus' conversations with them:

> As they were walking along the road, a man said to him, "I will follow you wherever you go."
> Jesus replied, "Foxes have dens and birds have nests, but the Son of Man has no place to lay his head."
> He said to another man, "Follow me."
> But he replied, "Lord, first let me go and bury my father."
> Jesus said to him, "Let the dead bury their own dead, but you go and proclaim the kingdom of God."
> Still another said, "I will follow you, Lord; but first let me go back and say goodbye to my family."
> Jesus replied, "No one who puts a hand to the plow and looks back is fit for service in the kingdom of God."

If we want to do God's will, we must not look back. Following God requires a stern stand and a forward focus. We must fix our eyes on Jesus. He is our Source of strength and encouragement. Following Jesus means that we must stand with Him amidst adversity and uncertainties.

During inhumane times, the slaves held to their faith in God. They believed that, although the forces of history were not on their side, God was. They kept their eyes on Jesus.

In the Jim Crow era, African Americans armed themselves with the strength that emancipated their ancestors from the clutches of slavery. The slave song, "I Shall Not Be Moved", became one of their theme songs. This song echoed a theology of audacious Christian tenacity and fortified their faith. In the face of overwhelming obstacles, Christians held on to Jesus. Crosses could not stop them, plantations could not tire them, and bombs could not destroy them. They were steadfast, unmovable, and continued faithfully in what they were convinced was the Lord's work (see 1 Corinthians 15:58).

Today, we enjoy some of the fruit of their tenacity.

They stuck with it even when the going got rough!

Let us learn from our ancestors and practice a *stick-to-itiveness* that depends on the Lord all the way.

Let us be encouraged as we reflect on these words of wisdom from King David:

> I keep my eyes always on the Lord. With him at my right hand, I will not be shaken. (Psalms 16:8)

TAKE A MOMENT TO REFLECT

Is there anything in your life that you find difficult to stick to?

Who will hold you accountable as you keep moving forward?

27

WADE IN THE WATERS...

God's gonna trouble the waters.

Wade in the water.
Wade in the water, children.
God's gonna trouble the water.

—"Wade in the Water", Negro spiritual

EVER FELT CHASED AND HAUNTED by your past? Ever felt like other people or things were assaulting your success? If so, you are in good company with slave history.

African-American slaves wanted freedom to live out the true meaning of their humanity. But no one else was willing to help them. The people who seemed to be in a position to help, for the most part, looked away. The few people who wanted to help them were limited in their willingness or ability to help. Many of the slaves set their eyes on freedom and believed they had within them what it took to gain that freedom. They did not believe that their condition was God's best for them.

Just as God led Israel out of Egypt through the water gateway of the Red Sea, they believed that He would bless them to arrive at freedom. It is widely noted that the slave's song, "Wade in the Water", was to some extent a tribute of faith to how they believed the Lord would bless them to gain freedom from their bondage.

Even more, "Wade in the Water" was a code song during escape attempts through efforts such as Harriet Tubman's Underground Railroad. At night, the slaves would launch an escape to freedom. When their slave masters heard about it, they pursued them with hound dogs to sniff out their paths. They would sing the song to signal to other slaves to get into the nearby waterway. In the water, the hound dogs would lose track of their human scent. This strategy proved to be effective. Many slaves got away to freedom by "wading in the water." The slaves believed that God had a plan for them, a better life than one of slavery and oppression.

Jeremiah 29:11 says,

"For I know the plans I have for you," declares the LORD, "plans to prosper you and not to harm you, plans to give you hope and a future."

Whenever God speaks, there are forces of opposition. They come in the forms of people, vices, attitudes, systems of oppression, and more.

You may be a victim of poor decisions, systems of opposition, addictions, or bad connections. Such vicissitudes can cripple progress toward a better life.

When I was in seminary at Candler School of Theology at Emory University, I served as a chaplain intern at a state prison in Atlanta. Each week, I looked into the faces of many brilliant people whose lives had been interrupted by one set of circumstances or another. The bigger challenge than their current incarceration was that many of them could not seem to see past it. From their pasts haunting them to focusing on the people who were to blame for their misfortune, their future was left dangling in the balance.

Before I dwell too much on the inmates at the state penitentiary, it is important to redirect the focus on you and me. Whether incarcerated or not, many of us often allow our pasts to hold us hostage from what our future holds. Some of us are incarcerated in mental prisons while we walk around looking free. Whenever we try to move beyond our pasts or beyond where we are now, oppression will come in various forms to try to pull us back or hold us down.

Slave history teaches us that we must be creative and not allow anything to hold us back or keep us down. We must have the audacity to resist resistance, deny denial, refuse to be refused, and reject rejection. Success is in the hands of those who trust God's will over their past and present circumstances.

To borrow from the last stanza of Maya Angelou's poem, "Still I Rise":

> Out of the huts of history's shame
> I rise
> Up from a past that's rooted in pain
> I rise
> I'm a black ocean, leaping and wide,
> Welling and swelling I bear in the tide.
> Leaving behind nights of terror and fear
> I rise
> Into a daybreak that's wondrously clear
> I rise
> Bringing the gifts that my ancestors gave,
> I am the dream and the hope of the slave.
> I rise
> I rise
> I rise.

Daring to rise in pursuing God's will against all odds sums up the audacious spirit of the song, "Wade in the Water." As you go throughout this day, keep in mind that God has a future and a hope that supersedes whatever challenges that try to keep you down, whether a physical or mental oppression.

Wade in the water. God is in the water to help you cross over to your destiny!

TAKE A MOMENT TO REFLECT

What are the influences in your life that keep you motivated to push through adversity?

_____

_____

_____

_____

_____

_____

What can you do to help others to overcome the oppressions of life to become all that God created them to be?

_____

_____

_____

_____

_____

_____

28

GIVE ME JESUS...

I heard my mother say; I heard my mother say; I heard
my mother say
Give me Jesus; Give me Jesus
You may have the world
Give me Jesus

Dark midnight was my cry; Dark midnight was my cry;
Dark midnight was my cry
Give me Jesus; Give me Jesus
You may have the world
Give me Jesus

In the morning when I rise; In the morning when I rise;
In the morning when I rise
Give me Jesus; Give me Jesus
You may have the world
Give me Jesus

—*"Give Me Jesus", Negro spiritual*

SOME NIGHTS ARE LONG and sleepless. Sometimes, situations
and people can hurt our feelings badly. The worst kind of hurt is
betrayal.

Betrayal is hard to deal with. It's the worst form of evil in many ways.

In the context of Jesus' Last Supper with his disciples, John 13:27 says, "As soon as Judas took the bread, Satan entered into him." Judas was on his way to betray Jesus to deliver Him into the hands of Roman soldiers to kill him. Jesus clearly discerned that Judas was staging his betrayal. Yet He turned to his disciples and taught them the power of love amidst the betrayal of a so-called friend, Judas!

In John 13:34-35, Jesus says,

> A new command I give you: Love one another. As I have loved you, so you must love one another. By this everyone will know that you are my disciples, if you love one another.

What a Word!

It is much easier to love someone who we don't know or even someone who we've never done anything to support. It is much harder to deal with the betrayal of someone we love and have drawn into our inner circle. It tears at the heart and causes many sleepless nights!

Yet amidst the heart-wrenching reality of Judas' betrayal, Jesus taught the rest of his disciples the power of unconditional love. In other words, this kind of love in the face of betrayal defines what it means to be one of Christ's disciples.

Jesus' experience of loving in the face of betrayal not only shows us how to be true disciples but also gives us reason to serve Him. We have a Lord and Savior who understands our pain. Because He can relate to the worst kind of emotional pain, Jesus is willing to be with us through our hurts, even in sleepless nights.

In the morning, He reminds us that there is another day on the other side of the darkness.

The song, "Give Me Jesus", was born out of deep physical and emotional turmoil. African-American slaves discovered that Christ-centered spirituality was like a healing balm that nursed the sores of their hearts. Soon, the night would give way to the morning. They celebrated the practical value that faith in Jesus brought to their aching hearts. All they could say was,

> Dark midnight was my cry; dark midnight was my
> cry; dark midnight was my cry
> Give me Jesus; Give me Jesus
> You may have the world
> Give me Jesus

> In the morning when I rise; In the morning when I
> rise; In the morning when I rise
> Give me Jesus; Give me Jesus
> You may have the world
> Give me Jesus

No wonder at Jesus' birth, the angels said, "Glory to the God in the highest!" The child Jesus was God on earth to bring peace to a troubled world.

In our most severe emotional and even physical pain, let's call Jesus. He is our peace. He is our joy.

"Give me Jesus!"

During some of the lowest points in my life, I have learned the power of Jesus' name. I have felt misled, betrayed, undermined, and left alone. Often, my shortcomings and failures blind me from feeling like a successful man. Time and time again, riding alone in my car, I have just whispered the name of Jesus.

Many nights, I have cried until the breaking of day. As the sun arose over the horizon, I was repeating the name of Jesus. I have found Christ to be a true friend!

May the power of Jesus' name be present in your life. May His peace calm you in your life's storms. May Jesus be your heart's healing salve.

"Give me Jesus!"

Take a Moment to Reflect

In what ways are you experiencing hurt? Remember that there is a balm in Gilead!

_____
_____
_____
_____
_____
_____
_____

Do you find it difficult to love those who have betrayed you? When will you trust God to heal?

_____
_____
_____
_____
_____
_____
_____

29
HOW I GOT OVER...

Whom shall I fear?

How I got over; How I got over, my Lord;
And my soul looked back and wondered
How I got over, my Lord.

The tallest tree in Paradise
The Christians call it tree of life;
And my soul looked back and wondered
How I got over, my Lord.

Lord, I've been 'buked and I've been scorned,
And I've been talked 'bout as sure as you're born;
And my soul looked back and wondered
How I got over, my Lord.

Oh, Jordan's river is so chilly and cold,
It will chill your body but not your soul;
And my soul looked back and wondered,
How I got over, my Lord.

 —*"How I Got Over", Negro spiritual*

HOW OFTEN DO YOU PAUSE to think about how far you have come? Ups and downs, but you made it. Frustrations and pain, but you made it. Maybe even oppressed or depressed, but we made it.

God has been there all the time!

"How I Got Over" was a Negro spiritual. Mahalia Jackson made the song famous as a theme song during the Civil Rights Movement. Jackson was born in New Orleans in 1911. She grew up in poverty, living in a shotgun house with 12 other people. Her Aunt Duke raised her after her mother died in 1917. Economic circumstances forced Mahalia to quit school and work at home when she was only in the fourth grade.[14] Undoubtedly, Mahalia Jackson's impassioned and Spirit-filled delivery was filled with her own relatability to the lyrics of the spiritual:

> How I got over; How I got over, my Lord;
> And my soul looked back and wondered
> How I got over, my Lord.

Sometimes, fear grips my heart. Anger builds up when things don't go the way I expect. Recently, I heard a still voice in my spirit saying, "Antipas, you are too far up in this." I understood the informal language. God was saying that I was getting in the way of what He was going to do.

Fear interferes with faith! Faith sets the platform for God to work in our lives. Fear causes us to waste energy and wears us out both mentally and physically.

Whom shall we fear?

God is on our side!

The Lord has proven Himself again and again. Current realities often blind us to the opportunity to rejoice that we made it *over*.

Slave Christians jolt our consciousness of how far we have come, the resilience with which we have journeyed and the victory we have won:

> Lord, I've been 'buked and I've been scorned,
> And I've been talked 'bout as sure as you're born;
> And my soul looked back and wondered
> How I got over, my Lord.

The days have been draining by life's sweltering heat. The nights have been long and cold. The slaves said it well:

> Oh, Jordan's river is so chilly and cold,
> It will chill your body but not your soul;
> And my soul looked back and wondered,
> How I got over, my Lord.

How amazing!

Look in the mirror. You do not look like what you have been through! The depth of the sorrow, the intensity of the crises, and the embarrassing failures only made you wiser and stronger.

It is in this vein that the Psalmist wrote,

> Praise the Lord, my soul;
>   all my inmost being, praise his holy name.
> Praise the Lord, my soul,
>   and forget not all his benefits—
> who forgives all your sins
>   and heals all your diseases,
> who redeems your life from the pit
>   and crowns you with love and compassion,
> who satisfies your desires with good things

so that your youth is renewed like the eagle's.
The Lord works righteousness
and justice for all the oppressed. (Psalms 103:1-6)

TAKE A MOMENT TO REFLECT

Reflect on the obstacles that, because of God's grace, you have overcome.

What are some of the lessons you have learned through life's experiences that have pushed you to become a better, wiser, and stronger person?

– 120 –

30

MY SOUL LOVES JESUS… BLESS HIS NAME!

My soul loves Jesus; my soul loves Jesus;
my soul loves Jesus, bless His name
My soul loves Jesus; my soul loves Jesus;
my soul loves Jesus, bless His name

He's a wonder in my soul; He's a wonder in my soul;
He's a wonder in my soul, bless His name
He's a wonder in my soul; He's a wonder in my soul;
He's a wonder in my soul, bless His name.

—*"My Soul Loves Jesus", traditional African-*
American congregational song

LIFE BRINGS MANY CHALLENGES as well as opportunities. In either case, God is faithful to stick with us. May we respond to God's faithfulness in caring for the spiritual nature of the soul.

Spiritual soul-care soothes the inner person and helps us to learn to appreciate opportunities and to remain resilient through challenges. Prayer, meditation, attending church, and other worship expressions such as singing and playing musical instruments are *spiritual* practices when the soul is in them.

One may think of soul as being the music of the heart. Going through the motions is not enough. Soul draws together human experience and a spiritual connection with God. Twentieth century theologian Dietrich Bonhoeffer calls the *Psalms* "the Prayer book of the Bible." One may note, along with Bonhoeffer, that David and the other psalmists constructed the *Psalms* in such a way that music draws upon the dance between life's experiences and deep communion, admiration, and at times, even wrestling with God. Bonhoeffer aptly noted,

> Prayer does not mean simply to pour out one's heart. It means rather to find the way to God and to speak with him, whether the heart is full or empty. No man can do that by himself. For that he needs Jesus Christ.[15]

Music of the heart to God is prayer from the soul. Praying from the soul is letting the music of the heart reveal the wonderment of our innermost being to God. The Holy Spirit helps us to pray from the soul with words that cannot be articulated clearly. Paul said,

> The Spirit helps us in our weakness. We do not know what we ought to pray for, but the Spirit himself intercedes for us through wordless groans. And he who searches our hearts knows the mind of the Spirit, because the Spirit intercedes for God's people in accordance with the will of God. (Romans 8:26-27)

Through the good and bad, hurts and joys, love and betrayals, victories and disappointments, the Spirit of Christ is there all the time. He remains faithful to us even when we are not faithful to Him.

When I think about Christ's deep love and faithfulness, it overwhelms me. The words of that ole worship song come to mind:

He's a wonder in my soul, bless His name.

King David spoke of the awestruck wonder of the Lord when he said,

Come and hear, all you who fear God, and I will tell what he has done for my soul. (Psalms 66:16)

Indeed, God cares for the soul!

As an act of gratitude for what God does for us, we must tend to our souls. Nineteenth-century Christian writer William Scott Downey said,

Would men take the same care of their souls as they do of their bodies, we should find our churches as thronged upon the Sabbath, as our markets are upon a Saturday.

We must be careful not to lose our souls. Downey is saying that it is possible to gain a lot but lose our souls. Jesus said,

What good will it be for someone to gain the whole world, yet forfeit their soul? Or what can anyone give in exchange for their soul? (Matthew 16:26)

Indeed, Jesus cares about what we do for our souls. And, loving Jesus means to glorify Him through soul-care. All too often, we relish in God's faithfulness but fail to tend to our souls.

Another 19th-century minister, Henry Ward Beecher, said, "The soul is often hungrier than the body, and no shops can sell it food."

As we go throughout our day, let's meditate on the Word of God. Only God can fill the hungry soul. Psalms 107:9 states,

> For he [God] satisfies the longing soul, and the hungry soul he fills with good things. (ESV)

Let's spend time praying and singing melodies in our hearts to the Lord (see Ephesians 5:19b).

May our souls love on Jesus!

TAKE A MOMENT TO REFLECT

Do you spend enough time with Jesus?

What can you do to keep Jesus first?

ENDNOTES

1. Stan Phelps, "Rethinking the Daily Grind: New Research Challenges Monday Morning Blues in the Workplace" in *Forbes*. Online: no page numbers.
http://www.forbes.com/sites/stanphelps/2015/04/23/rethinking-the-daily-grind-new-research-challenges-monday-morning-blues-in-the-workplace/ (Accessed December 24, 2015).

2. Charles P. Pollak, Michael J. Thorpy, and Jan Yager, "Monday Morning Bues," in *Encyclopedia of Sleep and Sleep Disorders* (3rd Edition), (New York: Facts on File, 2010), 134.

3. Chauncey W. Crandall, "Monday Morning Stress," in *Newsmax Health*. Online Source: No page numbers.
http://www.newsmax.com/Health/Dr-Crandall/article/2011/06/03/id/477014/ (Accessed, December 27, 2015).

4. Ibid.

5. TravelerIntoTheBlue, "Mississippi John Hurt - Monday Morning Blues." Audio Recording: No page numbers. https://youtu.be/zd3TpjWyVX0 (Accessed December 27, 2015).

6. Amy Oden (editor), "Madame Jeanne Guyon, Spiritual Torrents, (late 1600s)." From *In Her Words: Women's Writings in the History of Christian Thought* (Nashville: Abingdon Press, 1994), 246-247.

7. Howard Thurman, *Jesus and the Disinherited* (Boston: Beacon Press, 1976), 100.

8. Amy Oden (editor), "Catherine of Genoa, *The Spiritual Dialogue* (Late 1400s)." From *In Her Words: Women's Writings in the History of Christian Thought* (Nashville: Abingdon Press, 1994), 205.

9. Amy Oden (editor), "Jane de Chantal, *Letters of Spiritual Direction* (1625-39)", 233

10. Malcolm Gladwell, *Outliers* (New York: Back Bay Books, 2008), 267.

11. Ibid., 268.

12. Julian of Norwich, *Showings*, Chapter XXIV (Mahwah, NJ: Paulist Press, 1978), 167-68.

13. Emily Deans, "Stress: The Killer Disease: Stress and Inflammation Leave Us Vulnerable to Depression," in *Psychology Today*, November 26, 2012. No page numbers. https://www.psychologytoday.com/blog/evolutionary-psychiatry/201211/stress-the-killer-disease (Accessed, March 2, 2016).

14. Mahalia Jackson, "A Childhood in New Orleans." No page numbers. http://www.mahaliajackson.us/biography/ (Accessed, March 26, 2016).

15. Dietrich Bonhoeffer and Eberhard Bethge (editor), *Psalms: The Prayer Book of the Bible* (Minneapolis: Augsburg, 1970), 9-10.

CPSIA information can be obtained at www.ICGtesting.com
Printed in the USA
LVOW07s2359010416

481865LV00002B/3/P